PTSD

Understanding the effects of PTSD is a very complex and confusing process. The only thing modern medical technology can agree on is, PTSD is real. The medical world can't explain why it affects some and not others. This book is NOT a "How To" nor an attempt to offer a fix or cure.

The purpose of this book is to offer some insight into what a person struggling with PTSD can be facing. It is the author's attempt to let other veterans know they are not alone. In a number of cases, a suffering veteran can't articulate the events within their mind. Hopefully, the reader can come to terms with their issues by relating to the dark moments as described herein.

The second goal of this book is to give friends and love ones a vivid view of what a PTSD victim is struggling to deal with. Many veterans find it difficult to explain because they don't understand themselves. At times the veteran may be uncomfortable trying to relate such dark events. In other cases the veteran may feel guilty. The confusion and fears faced by anyone suffering from PTSD can cause an array of mental issues.

A person's perception of life changes as one ages. Age gives an individual more time to reflect on life's many challenges, both failures and successes. Combat Veterans are programmed to be strong and non-wavering in adverse times. Over time this wall of uncompromising strength may start to crumble. As a love one of a Combat Veteran, you may start to notice a change especially around holidays. Please keep in mind, to the vet, this change in strength and emotions can and will be confusing. To some it is more than they can deal with. If you have a Combat Veteran in your life, as a friend or relative, don't assume all is OK with them. Take the time to talk to them, visit them, get to know them, show them you really care!!

PTSD, especially among combat vets is something the military and government has ignored and denied throughout history. Only recently has the military and health care providers started acknowledging it.

At some point a Combat Veteran stood up for you, perhaps it's time you stood up for them!!

PTSD has been compared to grieving the loss of a love one.

Grieving, as defined in short burps

Grieving is like a drowning person, gasping for light but only seeing darkness
Grieving is when mentally you view reality as a nightmare
Grieving is yearning for what you know you can no longer have
Grieving is being alone among a crowd
Grieving is when you can smile on the outside and cry internally
Grieving is screaming at the world and no one hears
Grieving is seeking understanding, and finding only confusion
Grieving is reaching out, and feeling naught but a cold wind
Grieving is a frame of mind, a path, a journey, a place unknown, except to those that know it
Grieving is walking among the living, and living among the dead
Grieving is dying a slow death.

I stood among a vast surrounding not knowing where I am. The air felt chilled, yet warmed. Before me was a bright fog with trailing ends whirling like being blown by a great wind. Yet the air was still. It was eerie quiet. A soothing tranquility engulfed my mind. I stood frozen, not from fear, rather from the peacefulness of what my eyes saw or didn't see.

Another Day

Off in a distance I hear the sound
Of another day as it comes around
I see the clouds break open up in the sky
As the morning rays pierce my eyes

I reach for the warmness on my skin
And wish for the warmth to feel within
A cold and darkness envelopes me
Like a tidal wave rolling from the sea

I sit and listen to the children play
As they laugh and sing on their merry way
Their hearts so pure and minds so clear
No dreaded thoughts or blackened fear

I hear the sounds of another day
That I must face while on my way
I yearn for a time when my mind was free
But I know deep down, that's not to be

I have no reason to feel the way I do
As the clouds roll back and the sky turns blue
Life is grand, or it should be
But being alone sets the demons free

I hold them at bay as the day get brighter
But slowly and slowly the circle gets tighter
As the day starts to end and evening falls
I can hear their words, I hear them call

Off in a distance I hear the children sing
Innocent of all, life has to bring
Lightness fades as darkness prevails
And I prepare myself for another hell

The Mind

I gaze into my hollowed eyes and look into the
soul
The soul, like the mind, once so rich and bold
I am witnessing the complete destruction of the
heart, mind and soul

The intricate demolition of the many molecules
Which forms a functional being
The failure of the complex thought process
That allows rational thinking and normal day to
day activity

I am, through the eyes of one
Seeing the magnificent collapse of the single most
important trait
That separates a man from an animal
It is now shrouded in a concave mist of grey fog
A darkness of demons

A universe of unexplained confusion,
Where the mind no longer attempts to rationalize
A place where one can stand afar and witnesses
one's self

A world of parallel extremes
A division of one's mind and body
A path of complex and mesmerizing unison of
unknown reality

Where one can be and not be, each identical to the
other
An existence of two entities
One wrapped in a vale of authenticity
The other in a black void of insensitive
Uncaring and cold consciousness

A domain where one's action is justified
By one's aspiration
It is beautiful in its conception.
A journey not traveled, but for a few

A sight so elaborate one has to
Be insane to appreciate
The full scope of the
Devastation of a heart, mind and soul

As I Walk

As I walk this lonely road
In search of a life I've only known
I look about but to no avail
I'm roaming down an endless trail

All my past has come and gone
And in its wake, a shattered home
The future seems like a wasted task
As I stumble down this endless path

I look for hope in things I see
But everything is evading me
I know not where I now belong
My lonesome house is an empty home

My quest for life is eluding me
I no longer like what I see
I look at death in a different light
No longer do I see it as a fright

Death is a doorway we all must pass
But no longer is it a dreadful task
I view it as a way to go
How easy to walk through the threshold

Bad Day

It's going to be a bad day
I can feel it in my soul
It's going to be a bad day
And I have nowhere to go

It's going to be a bad day
My house is an empty home
It's going to be a bad day
As the demons start to roam

It's going to be a bad day
I hear the voices so clear
It's going to be a bad day
My demons are so near

It's going to be a bad day
I no longer have the will to fight
It's going to be a bad day
I no longer see the light

It's going to be a bad day
A friend trusted and I failed
It's going to be a bad day
When life becomes a hell

It's going to be a bad day
I hear the screaming in my mind
It's going to be a bad day
No peace can I find

Cold Lonely Night

Twas the night before Christmas
And I sit all alone
In a cold empty house
That once was a home

The stockings are hung
By the chimney with care
Remembering a time
When little ones were there

I sit in the darkness
A drink in my hand
The silence is roaring
Like a large marching band

Many many years ago
So different it would have been
With the laughter of children
And the faces of friends

The cheers have all fallen
Like an early winter snow
For no longer is there a spirit
Nor any place to go

No longer are there presents
Sounds of merriment in the air
Just these four lonely walls
As I sit in the dark and stare

Sun rise in the morning
Shall mark another day
For an old and lonely soul
Just wasting away

Desperation

No one really knows me
I don't even know myself
No one hears me screaming
As I reach out for help

No one really knows me
Or even tries to take the time
As the demons rip and roar
Through the crevices of my mind

Those close around me
Never bother to simply ask
They are blinded in their own world
And watches as the time slowly pass

No one really knows me
They never see my pain
No one ever hears me
Each day is just the same

I have tried to explain
But no one wants to know
The battles within me
As the demons claim my soul

Fantasy World

I live in a fantasy world
Where everyone seeks a dream
I live in a fantasy world
Where nothing is as it seems

Those who reside in this universe
We are all just the same
We have a hole within our soul
And we battle with our pain

I stand within a flowing crowd
No one around me can see
The loneliness within my heart
Or hear my mournful pleas

I walk a road of real despair
A frown upon my face
I search and search to no avail
To find a peaceful place

I live within a fantasy world
Where love is just a game
I seek to grasp reality
Before I go insane

I live within a fantasy world
A sad, sad place to be
Loneliness is my surroundings
That destiny has chosen for me

Fate

I look around at all that's here
But the retched sight I do not fear
The mournful sounds
And the hollowed faces come about from many
places

The path beneath my feet is weak
As I look around for what I seek
I see not now what lies ahead
For all around is lying dead

The trip I take is a grinding pace
And up ahead I see a face
A cheerful smile coming back to me
But its eyes I cannot see

Two doors before me suddenly appear
Neither one do I fear
For one I choose this very day
 Or in this hell I will always stay

Choose my path the door said to me
For I shall release and set you free
Your mind shall soar like never before
Comes the words to me from the big red door

It's I you want, say the door of green
For I know your eyes and what they've seen
Take my path and its journey ahead
Any but I and you'll end up dead

Off in a distance of a direction of three
I hear the words coming back to me
Tis I you want no other will do
The red and green will make you a fool

The groaning sounds behind I hear
As the walls close in and death draws near
I reach my hand to choose the door for me
When all a sudden I cannot see

For fate has finally --------- Caught up with me

Forgotten Heroes (VA Hospital)

I walked through the doors of glass
With its huge frames of steel
And gazed across a large room of humanity
Moving like waves of grain in an open field

The souls there were old, some tattered and worn
Some were in wheelchairs, others walked with
canes
One look into their eyes and it was plain to see
Each carried with him, their own bags of pain

Some moved about quite sharply
Other's gait was unsteady and slow
But each moved about their business
For they had no place to go

It came to me so quickly
It really should not have surprised
For it was a generations of Heroes
Standing right before my eyes

A band of forgotten soldiers
Battles still fought in their mind
A generation of living heroes
Now aged and thrown aside

They stood so straight and fearless
When they answered their nation's call
And now they are forgotten
As they walk among these halls

I stood so still and humble
In my mind I saluted all
Though old, tired, and beaten
These heroes never stood so tall

Hand of God

I touched the hand of God today
As I knelled down to pray
I felted his hand embracing mine
With a love so warm and kind

I touched the hand of God today
As he looked into my eyes
I touched the hand of God today
As my heart begun to cry

I never really saw his face
Though I could tell he was so near
I touched the hand of God today
As my eyes filled with tears

I felt the hand of God today
And to me he did say
Worry not and have no fear
For your time on earth is drawing near

I touched the hand of God today
I was engulfed by a peaceful heat
I touched the hand of God today
As I kneeled at his feet

Have You Ever Wondered

Have you ever wondered:
What it's like to not want to get out of bed

Have you ever wondered:
What it feels like to when your life is full of dread

Have you ever wondered:
Why these thoughts can go through your head

Have you ever wondered:
When it matters not, if you are alive or dead

Have you ever wondered:
The relief of finding someone again

Have you ever wondered:
The enlightment of discovering a true friend

Have you ever wondered:

I Am an Old Soldier

I am but an old soldier
Alone and misunderstood
I am but an old soldier
In harm's way I once stood

I am but an old soldier
My numbers are growing small
I am but an old soldier
I shall always stand tall

I am but an old soldier
I stood when my country called
I am but an old soldier
Many like me in time did fall

I am but an old soldier
I am so proud to say
I am but an old soldier
And will remain until my final day

I Fear Not Death

I've seen death's trail and followed its path
I've tasted its hard hand of wrath
My time draws near, too soon I know
When death will come and with it I'll go

Death is as real as God above
It's in this form he shows his love
If I had life to travel again
I would never accept death as a friend

It has a way of darkening your soul
Death turns your heart icy cold
I know it's there, it's always near
Death is not a thing to fear

I've been so close, I've seen its faces
Too many times, in too many places
I cannot wash away the blood stain sights
That continues to haunt me every night

Death is a sound as sweet as a lark
To a dying man afraid of the dark
I've tried to explain to those close to me
But they can't fathom what they can't see

They choose to ignore or fail to recognize
My hallowed tears and outward cry
Death is a peace we should not mourn
Death is life in a different form

I do not pity all before me gone
I envy not all yet called home
I begrudge not those who fail to understand
For death is personal to a dying man

Death can take my life, as he judges so
But only God, will claim my soul

I Gaze

I gaze out across the make believe
And stare into the life of me
I wonder where I went so wrong
These walls are no longer a merry home

I gaze into a darken world
Its paths and trails twists and swirls
It's blinding light burns my eyes
As panic sets in and it makes me cry

Deep in the crevices of my wayward mind
I seek a peace I cannot find
I yearn to walk in the morning light
But I sit in a darkness of a cold cold night

The time will come I know so well
When I no longer walk this path of hell
My peace shall come and I will find
A tranquil place within my mind

Death

I wish I could explain
The loneness within my soul
I stand among a crowd
But no one seems to know

My life has become a shamble
Not the way I meant for it to end
No longer do I have a family
So few do I call a friend

The demons from within
Haunt my every night
Their eyes control my mind
With a fearful sight

I struggle to stay sane
Whatever sane may be
When all I desire
Is to let my soul be free

I seek a simple peace
I'm willing to reap what I sow
But many fail to understand
They just do not know

My demise draws near
I welcome its embrace
I see death's flaming eyes
I see its haunting face

It Is What It Is

The words I speak they cannot hear
The syllables fall on deafen ears
I search about but do not find
A part of me that's really mine

Perception is reality
It is so real in my mind
To search the cauldron of darkness
Knowing the light I will not find

The vast expansion of time and space
Rips through my mind and leaves an empty place
I reach out to touch what is not there
I fail to hold, but I do not care

My path across life's many trails
Circle around to a life of hell

It Is What It Is
There's nothing else to say
It Is What It Is
And will remain until judgment day

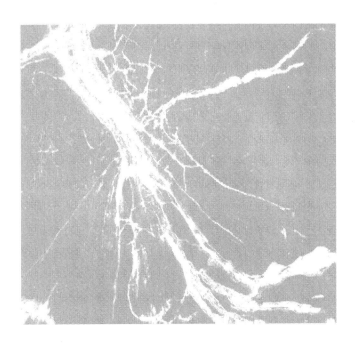

Life Takes Its Toll

I knew before my eyes opened
Before I rose from my bed
Tho I never can explain it
It is the demons in my head

I've long since quit fighting
The efforts are in vein
I brace myself for what's to come
The heartaches and the pain

Time is never good to a troubled mind
Age dimishes the soul
It breaks the will to mount a fight
It makes one's heart turn cold

I've lived my life as best I could
Many mistakes there has been
But never have I crossed the line
And violated the trust of a friend

Family has always been to me
The purpose of the seasons
But I have failed in my approach
For some unknown reason

Time has taken its dreadful toll
And again I sit here all alone
In a dark and chilling place
I now call a home

The demons creep within my mind
I can feel their haunting breath
And in their eyes of flaming red
I see the fear of death

Lonely Road

As I walk this lonely road
In search of a life I've only known
I look about but to no avail
I'm roaming down an endless trail

All my past has come and gone
And in its wake, a shattered home
The future seems like a wasted task
As I stumble down this endless path

I look for hope in things I see
But everything is evading me
I know not where I now belong
My lonesome house is an empty home

My quest for life is eluding me
I no longer like what I see
I look at death in a different light
No longer do I see it as a fright

Death is a door we all must pass
But no longer is it a dreadful task
I view it as a way to go
How easy to walk through the threshold

Looking Beyond

I sit in this foggy haze and stare beyond the
horizon of life
I gaze into a universe of peace and calm
Far outside the limits of my pain and demons
Lies the utopia of the human mind

I sense a faint breeze across my face
As the sweet smell of tranquility fills my soul
Across the darken boundaries of my existence
Lies the clarity of deliverance
Beyond restraints of material reality beckons my
spirit

The path lies at my feet
Authenticity of a serene sleep is but one step away

No One Seems To Mind

It seems so strange
The things I see
Rolling through my mind

I know each segment of my thoughts
Borders on the final drop.
I can stand back and watch from afar

I watch my mind and soul separate
From my very being
I can reach out and touch
But cannot feel

I am different and so departed
I walk away and not look back
Never to return.

No Time

You've never felt my sadness
You've never seen my tears
Nor seen life through my eyes
Or know my demons and my fears

You know so little about me
Even though you think you do
You judge me so severely
It makes my world so blue

My life has become expendable
No time in your world, for me
I'm toss aside and forgotten
Like a ball on the open sea

No longer do you visit
My phone has ceased to chime
My life has become expendable
You no longer have the time

The air that fills your lungs
Is the wind that guides my soul
My life has become expendable
I feel the depths of its cold

The heart that beats within your chest
Is the same that beats in mine
My life has become expendable
Because you haven't the time

My days are very limited
When the sunrise will no longer shine
My life has become expendable
Because you no longer have the time

When my final verse is written
No more breath will I find
Shed no tears over my body
Because you haven't the time

No Where to Go

I cave into the evil thoughts
That scourges through my mind
I drift about the lonesome path
As life leaves me behind

I stand so firm, like an old oak tree
But no matter what I say
No one will ever notice
As my soul fades away

I slowly slide beneath the lines
Of a reality seen only by me
Into a blackened cauldron
Beneath a boiling sea

A sea of vast perspective
Where my mind cannot thrive
A sea of darken demons
Where a sane mind cannot survive

In a clouded haze of confusion
Where thoughts have no bounds
In a world of mass trepidation
Where words have no sounds

I return to this haunted place
In search for what, I do not know
I shall roam until eternity
For I have nowhere to go

Notice

No one will ever notice
The day that I die
They will be some that mourns
And a few will even cry

The voices around me
And the feet walking by
Will never really notice
The day that I die

Lying in a crowded house
I suspect I will die all alone
With people all around
Sitting in an empty home

The world I once lived in
With laughter and love abound
Has slowly crept through my fingers
And no one comes around

I no longer see their faces
No matter how hard I try
No one will ever notice
The Day that I die

Sleep

If home is where your heart is
Mine is buried six foot down
If home is where your heart is
Mine is in the cold hard ground

I try to see beyond the dark gray mist
And look at a bright blue sky
I try to rise from this blackened hole
As time slowly drifts on by

I fight the demons within my soul
A battle I can't seem to win
I stand and look them in the eye
In a war that will never end

My home is not as home should be
No matter what I try
My home is not as my home should be
And it brings tears to my eyes

I wonder not why I am this way
No pity do I seek
I wish only to lay down my head
For an eternal sleep

Son Rise

I rose early this morning
For it was the sun rise I wished to see
I rose early this morning
To acknowledge what this day means to me

I rose early this morning
And looked upon the sky
I rose early this morning
To behold the sun rise with my eyes

I rose early this morning
In my heart I felt an angel say
The Son has Risen
Christ lives this very day

Now the Son has Risen
With his forgiveness and his love
Now the Son has Risen
And shines down from heaven above

The Darkness of My Soul

I lie upon the edge of reality and stare
into the abyss. I pull the cover of darkness over me
like a child covers with a blanket.
The darkness blocks the mind and hides the light
of reality. But the darkness also brings
with it the demons that rules the night

The demons roam the pits of the unlighted
regions of the mind. Reality and the brightness
that controls those things the mind cannot let go.
One seeks a balance. A place between the light of
reality and the cold depths of the unlighted.

He, who finds this place, finds the peace sought by
all. A place that affords a calmness, a tranquility
unknown to the mortal soul. A utopia in the
middle of one's crisis.

I cover myself in darkness. Where the demons of
my soul roam free
Seeking but not finding. Reaching out but not
grasping. Yearning, but not feeling
I face what is there, the eyes of the demons that
own my soul

I cover myself !!!!!!!!!!!!!!!!!

The Demons

The demons within my spirit
Come creeping from my soul
And stands right before me
So brilliant and so bold

The light that shines within my life
That casts a redeeming glow
Slowly fades into darkness
As I feel the chill of death's cold

Tis the season to be jolly
Singing of the children I do hear
As the memories of the past
Still rings in my ear

I reach out with my fingers
To absorb a spark of the times
Only to find a numbness
That consumes my very mind

I stand in the darkness
The cold air like a north wind
As life whirls around me
Cascading places I have been

The sounds are ever so haunting
As I stare into their eyes
The smell of death around me
As I slowly begin to die

Eyes

The darkness drapes around me like a blanket on a baby. The night chill penetrates my soul and my body shivers from its touch. I listen to the stillness of the air as my mind races. The quietness of the black void I dwell roars in my head

I reach to touch that which I cannot hold
I try to wrap my arms around a vast empty hole
I strain to see, though I am blind
I yearn to have again that which was mine

My body and my mind are frozen in a different time
I wish to run, but there's nowhere to hide
I am caught in a cauldron of confusing twists of ricocheting flashes in my mind
I seek a truth I shall never find

I look in vain, but cannot see
The haunting eyes, staring back at me
I breathe but yet I am not alive
My death came when I saw those eyes

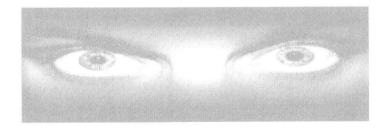

The Line of Life

I stand, straddling the fine line between the reality
seen by most and the darkness known but to a
few. It is very strange, at least to me, the ability to
see both so clearly. I see life, its familiar
surroundings as people come and go. I see its
stresses and strains of the day to day normal
activities. I see its failings, the pain and confusion.
But what I see is reality; it is just life as seen by all.
Then I gaze across the fine line that possesses half
of my existence.

I see a dark void full of brightness. It's a
contradiction of mental concept. I sense all around
me, though the darkness fills the air. I can see,
however I can't see. In my mind I am fully aware
of my surrounding as one would be on a warm
sunny day. But I am consumed in a cold darkness.
The astonishing revelation is the inability of
anyone to see or become aware of the vision that
lies before me. I am yet I am not!!
How can no one see the torment is a puzzle to me?
Perhaps I hide the trail so well. The path from my
soul leads to the pits of hell.

Tis a Grand Day to Die

Gather round all my men
And set your sights on high
For the time has come to set about
Tis a grand day to die

Gather round, all that will
For the battle is oh so near
Stand steady all my friends
For there is nay a reason to fear

Lock and load and cinch up tight
And kiss the ladies good-bye
For the time has come among us
On this grand day to die

The demons that set our souls afire
And makes the weak ones cry
Stands before us in battle dress
Tis a grand day to die

No more noble a cause is there
Than to raise your saber high
And face death's troubling ways
On this grand day to die

Fear not what tomorrow brings
Stare today straight in the eye
For it is now that must be dealt with
On this grand day to die !!!!!

Toast

Here's to all my fallen friends
Who died while in their prime
We owe to you our gratitude
For the price you had to pay

I hoist my glass this very day
Like so many days before
To give to you, the homage due
In this simple way

The life you gave
Was the price you paid
But your memory shall
Never Fade

Troubled Soul

I sit alone in the pouring rain
Moisture dripping off my brow
I hear the demons of my soul
With their low and fearful growl

It's in my mind they come for me
The world is black within my soul
I no longer fear their burning eyes
The air about me is bitter cold

My life's journey has no beginning
As I stroll through the clouded trails of my mind.
The ending is but a concept of thought
I wander aimlessly in the black void of time

A realm of slipping reality
Mixed with fantasizing mind altering dreams
The demons of my mind grow closer
And I sense their chilling screams

Behold an abyss with the softness of a butterfly
As I glaze into a darken sea
I seek to reach out and touch
The things that were not to be

The past shall always haunt me
And fill the voids of my mind
The future is shrouded in darkness
Where the light will never shine

I am destined to always wander
With no home to ever go
I roam the wilderness of hell
No peace for a troubled soul

When my next tomorrow fails to arrive
The next sunrise fails to strike my face
I shall depart this realm with a gleeful heart
Finally having arrived at a peaceful place

Whiskey, Straight and Neat

Have a drink on me boys,
Make it whiskey, straight and neat
Gather all the children around, boys;
Have them sit down at your feet

Tell them of the times we've had,
And the many things we've done
Tell it all to them, boys
The good, the bad and the fun

Tell them of the many tales,
So that each and all will know
Tho gray and bend we are now,
Like them we once weren't old

Tell them of the beautiful ladies
 That still dances through our mind
Who's loving smile and warming touch,
Is no longer ours to find

Have another drink boys,
Just let the whiskey flow
Have this round for me boys,
And then just let me go

Whiskey straight and neat, boys,
Shall be my last request
As they lower me down into the ground,
I'll finally get to rest

Winds

I stare into the winds of death
As the dust of life slowly settles ore' my soul
The stench that follows, burns my eyes
I stand so firm, for I have nowhere to go

I once pondered my nightly dreams
And wished they all came true
But life has taught me a troubling lesson
Nightmares are dreams too

The walls of destiny surround me
As I glaze upon the haunting eyes
The demons of my past comes forward
I hear their wailing and their cries

I wish I could explain
The nightmares of my mind
Then perhaps others would understand
The peace I seek to find

My regrets are but a few
No pity do I crave
No one can truly judge me
For my nightmares, I take to my grave

In life, the most valuable asset a person possesses, next to health, is time. Taking your time to read my book is tantamount to you giving me a gift of your time. I sincerely appreciate this gift.

If you have any comments, please contact me at: Sterling849@yahoo.com

Terry Dailey

Terry has several books published you might find interesting.

The Literary World of a Simple Man
   This book shares some of the material outlined here

A Mercenary's Story

Revenge is Never Sweet

These books can be found on: Amazon.com

Made in the USA
Columbia, SC
02 July 2024

37994780R00030